Dirge for an Imaginary World

DIRGE
FOR AN
IMAGINARY WORLD

POEMS BY
Matthew Buckley Smith

WINNER OF THE 2011 ABLE MUSE BOOK AWARD

ABLE MUSE PRESS

Copyright ©2012 Matthew Buckley Smith
First published in 2012 by

Able Muse Press

www.ablemusepress.com

All rights reserved. No part of this book may be used or reproduced in any manner whatsoever without written permission except in the case of brief quotations embedded in critical articles and reviews. Requests for permission should be addressed to the Able Muse Press editor at editor@ablemuse.com

Printed in the United States of America

Library of Congress Control Number: 2011944931

ISBN 978-0-9878705-0-6

Foreword copyright ©2012 by Greg Williamson

Cover image: *The Singing Flame* by Talon Abraxas

Cover & book design by Alexander Pepple

Able Muse Press is an imprint of *Able Muse:* A Review of Poetry, Prose & Art—at www.ablemuse.com

Able Muse Press
467 Saratoga Avenue #602
San Jose, CA 95129

Acknowledgments

Thanks first to the editors of the following magazines, where versions of these poems have appeared:

"At the Spring Ballet Exams," "Heals-Gebedda," "Miss Americus," *Able Muse;* "On Being Naked," "For the Highway Medians," *Alabama Literary Review;* "Elegy with Bradford Pear Trees," *Beloit Poetry Journal;* "Converts," "Ars Poetica," "Notes on a Vermeer," *Blue Unicorn;* "Prothalamium for my Father," *The Chimaera;* "Late Aubade," *Commonweal;* "Bedding Procrustes," "Meaning," *Deronda Review;* "Juglans Nigra," *Innisfree Poetry Journal;* "Nowhere," *Iron Horse Literary Review* and *Best American Poetry 2011;* "The Open House," *Linebreak;* "For the Girls Who Dance on Tables," *The Lyric;* "For the College Football Mascots," "When It Happens," *Measure;* "For the Neanderthals," "Letter in a Bad Time," *The Raintown Review;* "Youth," "A Lesson," "House-Sitting," *The Same;* "An Old Song," *Sewanee Theological Review;* "Benediction," *Slapering Hol Press Newsletter;* "Diary," "Atalanta's Wedding Night," *Think Journal;* "The Homemaker's Song," "Widows," *Unsplendid;* "Paradiso XIV, 63," *Vineyards;* "Inaudible Elegy," "A Message," *Wormsbook.*

Many thanks to Alex Pepple, the tireless editor of this book. Thanks to John Irwin, Mary Jo Salter, Dave Smith, and Greg Williamson, my teachers in the Johns Hopkins Writing Seminars. Thanks to the Foundation Fellowship of the University of Georgia and to Elizabeth Brient, Brian Henry, and Reg McKnight, my professors and guides at UGA. Thanks to everyone at the Paideia School, especially Clark Cloyd, Joseph Cullen, and Paul Hayward. Thanks to Alisan Atvur, Brendan Carnes, John Huss, Arthur Koch, and David Prude, steadfast friends all. Thanks especially to Ryan Wilson; this book is yours as much as it is mine. Never enough thanks to my wife, Joanna Pearson, my first reader, my favorite talker, my undeserved happiness.

Last, thanks to all of my family—broken and whole, new and old, living and dead.

Foreword

In this deeply impressive debut volume of poetry, *Dirge for an Imaginary World*, Matthew Buckley Smith delivers a remarkable range of deft formal schemes, temporal movements, and varied settings. We encounter sonnets, couplets, quatrains, Sapphics, sestets and so forth written with a slick, delightful merging of technical expertise and smooth contemporary rhythms. The range of subjects is equally and as charmingly eclectic, from Neanderthals, Dante, Vermeer, for instance, to College Football Mascots, Highway Medians, and Spring Ballet Exams.

Beyond the skillfulness and charm of the individual poems, themselves, one quickly comes to admire the thematic trajectory of Mr. Smith's arrangement. The book begins with what might at first be seen as less overtly personal poems: youth, caveman, myth, history, art, poetry, song. But as we read further we realize the canny way they are setting up imagined, mythic origins of a self-aware, self-suspicious even, twenty-first century poet.

The book continues on this arc as it becomes gradually more complexly introspective. For instance, the poem "A Lesson" puns intriguingly on the title. Set retrospectively in a college physics class, it questions the formulae, as it were, of youthful romance, its dissolution, what to make of it, and how it all adds up, or perhaps even if it did: "Erasing all we struggled to compose." Or this riddling question at the end of "House Sitting": "What would I not now lose, not to have lost/ That borrowed key we shared that week or two."

That kind of mental and linguistic agility, that generous challenge to the reader, happen in poem after poem. And since I might not have the right way to say it and don't want to give away the ending, I'd better let him tell it for himself through these gifted and winning poems.

—Greg Williamson

CONTENTS

Foreword ix

Youth 5

I.

For the Neanderthals 9
Bedding Procrustes 10
Atalanta's Wedding Night 11
Epitaph for Dionysus 12
Ars Poetica 13
To the Unknown God 14
The Ascetic Speaks of Heaven 18
Paradiso XIV, 63 19
Benediction 20
Night 21
Faith 22
Meaning 23

II.

Notes on a Vermeer 27
On Being Naked 28
A Lesson 29
An Old Song 30

House-Sitting 31
A Pledge 32
Elegy with Bradford Pear Trees 33
Converts 36
Diary 37
Juglans Nigra 38
For the Girls Who Dance on Tables 39
A Message 40
Prothalamium for My Father 41
Heals-Gebedda 42
Black Bile 43
The Open House 44
Before a Wedding 45

III.

Natural History 49
For the College Football Mascots 50
Anvil Way 51
When It Happens 52
Middle Age Toasts the End of Youth 53
Letter in a Bad Time 54
Late Aubade 55
Inaudible Elegy 56
The Homemaker's Song 57
Widows 58
For the Highway Medians 59
Nowhere 60
Miss Americus 61
First Love's Divorce 62
Priam's Dream 63
At the Spring Ballet Exams 65

Das Nichts selbst nichtet.

Heidegger

Dirge for an Imaginary World

Youth

I miss believing that I'll never die,
Or is it that there won't be a tomorrow?
Both lines work out about the same: deny
The day you'll have to pay back what you borrow.
It used to be I never went to bed
A second night with any girl I found.
No breakfast in those days—a smoke instead,
Then out the door before she came around.
Last night I passed a toppled garbage bin,
Its liner sagging with a rat's remains.
He sank a little when I squinted in
And seemed embarrassed by his greedy pains.
And so much like a man, the way he sat
Still in his death, and so much like a rat.

I.

For the Neanderthals

When you were nothing but dull-witted, wayward cousins,
We missed you less—believing you were unaware
Of what was happening, of the unlikely reasons
You'd be replaced. We liked to think you free of care.
That was your role: our stout, thick-snouted kin. Ill-fated
But oblivious, you fed and dozed and mated.

Then someone took another glance at what you left
And found your skulls allowed for brains as big as ours,
Or bigger, making room for fleeting dreams and deft
Apologies on deathbeds richly spread with flowers.
In desert chambers lay the artifacts of pain
You must have felt at losing those you knew you'd join.

Of course we also learned you dragged slick leaves of flint
Across the bones of your own tribe, to strip the meat.
You mastered fire, you cooked. Maybe you even spent
Odd empty moments sulking, feeling desolate.
We've done much worse, and better, in our hopeful age,
Strutting our share of hours and more upon the stage.

I've thumbed through color photographs of crumbling tools
And like to think I understand those minds that gave
Form to the world the way our own minds do. What fools
We were to tiptoe from the darkness of your cave,
Leaving you there to murmur God's name in a tongue
That died before it could evolve beyond a song.

Bedding Procrustes

Ruler me ruthlessly: metatarsal, brainpan, finger-bone.
    I came this far alone
With you in mind. In lust, inadequate, and lost.
    At any cost
I lay me down,
    From blistered sole to shaggy, dandered crown,
To pay the debt I've carried all my life
    And brought to you, my executioner, my wife.
Unknowable as Fate, you beckon,
    Fluffing a scabby pillow as you reckon
Distances traveled, heights defeated, lines surpassed
    In search of you, my weigh station, my last
Room, board, and long night's rest.
    I've come to terms with all my brethren and confessed
My faults to every priest but you.
    We're overdue.
No need for shackles, sleeping pills, or lies;
    Turn back the sheets and cut me down to size.

Atalanta's Wedding Night

Now that you've won my hand and come to claim the rest,
   I'll tell you what those other young men guessed

As they lay panting, beaten, on my father's track
   And watched me smile and—smiling—turn my back.

Among the dust and olive trees they must have felt
   Some doubt before the fatal stroke was dealt:

Could this, the girl to whom they'd lost, and wagered all,
   Be she who wept at Meleager's fall?

My husband and my champion, Hippomenes,
   I'm yours, and you're the one who's mine to please.

Still, know that when I stooped, and let you pass, and lost,
   It wasn't for the shining fruit you tossed,

But Meleager's fiery dying made me doubt,
   Three times, my heart, and reach to put it out.

Epitaph for Dionysus

God the lightning midwifed and planted
Safe in a heaven then brought again to term,
    What has undone you?

You, who've cut paths into the seamless
Winding sheet of snowfall that old men speak of
    As they are dying,

You've now joined the arms you commanded
Bared in winter, sleeved with blood in midsummer,
    Hacked from the skeptic.

Love, marooned and heartsick, once caught you
Fast in her sunburnt limbs, till your hand yielded
    Starlight to crown her.

Was it then you thought of your mother,
Ablaze with insight, leaving the careless world
    Nothing to bury?

Ars Poetica

O Muse, when I am dead as you
And done with begging grace and time,
My buried money turned to slime
And all my charms rehearsed away,
Which seemed like many, being few,
Then let my name return to clay,

And though stars gutter, while I live
Don't let what flickers flicker out,
But choke the whispers that would shout,
No work redeems what time will end.
And till I've come to ruin, forgive,
O Muse, the fortune that I spend.

To the Unknown God

> Ye men of Athens, I perceive that in all things ye are
> too superstitious. For as I passed by, and beheld your
> devotions, I found an altar with this inscription,
> TO THE UNKNOWN GOD. Whom therefore
> ye ignorantly worship, him declare I unto you.
>
> Acts 17:22-23

1.

Homeless, we come daily to Your gate,
Where the gossip turns to alms and bread.
Paper-colored palms' forgotten fronds
Clog the gutter's teeth. No word comes down.
Which of us has not wished back an hour
So that he might strike the offered cheek?
Mark our heads, unwashed, with eyes that drink
Only darkness from the bonfire's rim,
While your windowpanes reflect the bright,
Pillared smoke we took at first for light.

2.

That first death—maid, uncle—sets the world
One has hardly known beyond one's yard
Toppling, and all promises of youth
Sag within the child's hot, bee-stung view,
Public as the picnic afternoon
When a grownup brings the end to life:
Gone forever, always, yes, you, too.
Then an ice-cream float or game of catch,
Anything one asks for got, all day,
But this cup, please, taken back away.

3.

Scriptures, sermons, service-bells, and songs
Stretch to fill the empty tracts: Your will,
Read aloud by clerks amid the wake
Of the last surviving heir it names.
One discovers in a smoke-lit verse
Not conversion but an echoed call
Heard and heeded centuries ago
By unsteady, homesick fishermen
Who set out to map a promised land
Out of reach and always just at hand.

4.

One may call on You so seldom now
Outside the occasions love contrives
For a word, in loss, or out of hope,
Spoken by the dying for the dead
To recall the rumors of Your will...
Absent these, You grow so little known
Quiet rooms like these become You best.
Faced at evening with an empty glass,
Few make out the cipher of Your name,
Passing darkly as it darkly came.

The Ascetic Speaks of Heaven

Alive, I'd never have foreseen
The symmetry of paradise,
Youth's brimming cup at last serene,
   The overflow ice.

No pretty girls refresh the grave;
No cigarettes are saved hereafter.
One has no choice but to behave,
   Sans spirits and laughter.

Among the blessed, one pities those
Who lived for pleasure. Reminiscing
Over the plucked days, each one knows
   Exactly what he's missing.

Paradiso XIV, 63

Even in heaven, then, there is desire:
For resurrection in the appointed time,
When out of blackened earth new flesh will climb
Beyond the cross of every storm-whipped spire
Into that harmony kept by the choir
Assigned each soul, whose naked pantomime
Clothes itself there in joy, like sense in rhyme,
Like lyrics in the plucking of a lyre;

For this, but also for the body's own
Relentless, unrepentant want—to feel
Cool water on the brow, to bend and kneel
Within the house where skin and hair and bone
Meet in a smoky, sniffling, crassly real
Desire to live and not to be alone.

Benediction

Walking at dawn, I think I understand
What brought the ancients to that pale horizon.
How awful—and how perfect—to demand
You show Your face, the sun, against all reason.
Why wouldn't our lonely predecessors find
A tender sermon in the raveled fern,
A scripture in the workings of the hand,
In starlight grace no reason can discern?
We name ourselves, our fathers, our desires,
And so did they, the sweet, befuddled dead.
We should be grateful for their hopes, the fires
From which we've lit our own, the names they said
You answer to, the prayers You can't resist,
We who so seldom beg You to exist.

Night

Starting awake I'm like a man who waits
In line all day to pay a fee and—just
When he has finally reached the counter—doubts
Himself and limps off, cursing the time he's lost.
How is it, every year of my brief hours,
I've believed Thou art in heaven, hallowed,
Only to find myself now between doors,
Bolted, alone, hearing my small prayers bellowed
Back in a mocking echo? Well, I have,
And all the dreams and memories I've kept
Pass in my sleepless vision like a wave
Of heat across a public road. Christ wept
For Lazarus, and Lazarus, he spills
His tears for everyone, everyone else.

Faith

Maybe the glass I raise was drained
Two thousand years ago. Maybe I know
The friends I toast are gone, their bread consigned
To where, despite the grace of God, I'll go.
Wanting reply, my correspondence grows
Halfhearted, repetitious. What it lacks
In promise it makes up in compromise,
A new wick swallowing the same old wax.
The congregation yawns with empty places.
The hour strikes only when we least expect.
His shoes untied, the aging rector laces
Into shadows, eyes shut, gaze direct.
Maybe my hope the mysteries will resume
Is seed cast, fondly, to a barren womb.

Meaning

The soul mistakes the body for itself
And so despairs. Watchful, the body stirs,
Quick to divert its restless better half
With leisure's griefs and work's indifferent cures.
Sleepless, it never truly eats its fill;
Famished, it cannot slake its vacant lust;
Tumid and sore, it lies awake until
Daybreak can grant the crowing cock's request.
Such pastimes help time pass until they don't:
The milk goes rancid in a brand-new carton;
The weary lover one night simply won't;
Old songs that used to comfort now dishearten.
The soul begins to contemplate the soul,
A part that's not, and never will be, whole.

II.

Notes on a Vermeer

The painting is a place
Besides the one we frame.
The latter crowds have seen
On grounds a book can name.

The former, like a face
One passes in a store—
That labors by, unselfed—
Few notice anymore,

Besides the ones who grew
To artless age in view
Of women paid to clean
On such a street in Delft.

On Being Naked

The cemetery near the art school slept
A mossy, dreamless sleep, haunted by gnats;
Blunt headstones listed down the hill and crept
Further each moment from the world's regrets.
Not so for us, as friends and lovers of
The art school's rising stars. Long, chilly nights
Inside their studio, we stood for love,
Or sat, or sprawled, beneath fluorescent lights.
Loosed from our pride, our reason, and our clothes,
We giggled at ourselves and one another,
Reduced to what we'd always been, but chose
To hide: frail sister, soft and pallid brother.
At dawn, we'd share last cigarettes and sigh
To watch the trees undress the blushing sky.

A Lesson

It lasted one semester, maybe less;
    We met in physics class
    And parted ways for good
On campus, underneath a cottonwood.

Our stuttering teacher chalked with his right hand
    Each formula he planned
    To teach us, while the left
Rubbed all his work away in idle theft.

For weeks we dozed and never touched a book.
    What shallow breath it took
    Just to get up and dressed
Was all that we could muster at our best.

When was it we embraced our little loss?
    Pale sunlight fell across
    Our feeble, tender throes,
Erasing all we struggled to compose.

An Old Song

      Restless nights after class
      We'd sit down with a beer
To watch bicycles float by the bars
And the street's surface flicker like glass
      At a place we called ours
      For a week, or a year.

      With a little girl's smile
      You'd drop ash on my arm
And blow smoke at the papers I rolled.
Getting lit we passed off as a style
      And believed, or were told,
      We meant nobody harm,

      Till one night at our table
      You borrowed my knife
To cut four letters into the wood...
And I tried, but I just wasn't able,
      To pretend you'd be good
      For the rest of your life.

      Though we called the place ours
      For a year, or a day,
When the lights came on we had to pay.
All the shop windows glittered like stars—
      There was nothing to say,
      And there's nothing to say.

House-Sitting

Brief as it might have been, that week or two
Your art professor trusted you enough
To leave his home, his dogs, and all his stuff
Under the watch of such a one as you,

And by extension such a one as me,
That week has lingered, windows curtained, since
We played his warbling records, thumbed his prints,
Made off with love amid his cutlery,

Delighted in his bathtub, turning blue
Wherever skin and bare fluorescence crossed.
What would I not now lose, not to have lost
The borrowed key we shared that week or two?

A Pledge

What does it have to do with me today,
The hour or so we spent, ten years ago
And over seven hundred miles away,
Naked and still beside the traffic's flow?
A costume party weltered on behind us,
Garlanded figures raced about the pool,
And fireworks whistled brightly to remind us
We'd finished with our sheltered life at school.
There in the moss and monkey grass and gravel
Each car that thundered by tossed back our hair.
Some honked before continuing their travel
On to the night's engagements, God knows where.
Squinting against their headlights in the dust,
We made a pledge you might recall. You must.

Elegy with Bradford Pear Trees

Athens, Georgia

Their crooked boughs in bloom almost to rupture,
Pear trees shudder the length of the street.

Our windows are down and swallowing
Facefuls of warm damp twilight air

Ripe with the trees' uncanny stink.
How stupid I felt when you told me:

Semen—it was semen they smelled like!
Who wouldn't recognize his own reek?

And again I felt stupid, slowly seeing:
Of course, of course it would be you.

A little rain or breeze is all it takes
Gently to stipple sidewalks, cars, and sky

White in blossoms enough we might
Not recall whole surfaces of earth

Naked as they were before the spill.
We might not, but we do.

Remembering is why you've left
Down the windows and twirled up

The college station, scattering conversation.
Even before I knew what else it meant

Come was the best of all possible words,
At once suggesting *you* and *here* and *I*

Want you to. Even then. I want you to
Speak with your good sulking mouth

Again to me. Simply to make your lips part
I ask for the single best word you know.

You say *part*. And nearly twist the knob off
The radio, where Jeff Mangum's ghost is

Singing: *Semen stains the mountain-tops.*
Once, and then again, as if explaining,

Semen stains the mountain-tops,
Briefly convincing me something

Even as obscene as what my body makes
Calmly gleams, maybe, in another world,

Although he wrote those words in Athens,
Here in the piedmont. Here in the lowest

Rank of mountain there is nothing
Lofty to speak of. No pinnacles. No snow.

But maybe far enough away
Anything's simple enough to seem lovely:

The night iconic only in hindsight, the kiss
Good luck at the end of our drive,

The pear trees quaking at rumors of the wind.
Scentless in memory, still the clustered petals

Quicken at the tip of every branch. Even now
They quicken and come beautifully apart.

Converts

Learning all at once the gooseflesh Braille
Of one another's bodies, we couldn't turn
The pages fast enough, incanting parts
In foregone syllables from other tongues,
From places we had never seen, from times
We'd never led each other through. Purblind,
We groped with slippery hands the living text,
Taking to heart whole favorite passages
We'd not yet understood—and never would.

Diary

Some days I wake up easy, bathe, and dress
Before the sun has even shown its face.
Some days I stroll around the block and guess
The cause for every call the sparrows place.
Some days I smile at strangers and their kids,
I give my time and cigarettes unbidden,
I tip the clerk although a sign forbids
The gesture and the day before I didn't.
Some days I don't ignore the dirty clothes
Encroaching from the corners of my room,
I don't spend hours attempting to compose
A note, then tear it up, and then resume.
I do not drink alone, or punch the wall
Until it cracks, or think of you at all.

Juglans Nigra

    We had no words for what we found
Taking the air behind your house that night:
    Speckled with idle window light,
        Something pale green and round.

    Smooth to the touch and cold as stone,
It gave no scent. We passed it hand to hand,
    Laughing, and could not understand
        What little we'd been shown.

    Years later and too late I learned
How a black walnut looks and how it holds
    Its heavy fruit within its folds
        And how it must be earned.

For the Girls Who Dance on Tables

In fall as warm as bath water, the strip mall hints
At something past the city's asphalt rim, beyond
The business hours kept by the Chinese restaurants.
Radio towers accepting messages respond
In flashes to a dark and empty sky, while you
Wait for a drink, a laugh, some courtesy you're due.

It will not come, or if it will, then not tonight.
Tonight the regulars are nursing sober rounds
Of pool, sad, half-drunk beers held close. Not one will light
Your cigarette, or play the song you clap your hands
Begging to hear, to have a good time to. Not now.
You've charged as much already as the rules allow.

Behind the bar reclines a mirror. Do not look
There for resolve, for anything but years of rust
Drifting across that false room like a strip of yolk
Over a sizzling pan, like milk, like breadcrumbs tossed
By children to a flock of geese. Like none of these.
Don't look there as you wag your gentle breasts and knees.

You must be here, and we must be beside you here.
If not, we would be home, we would be going home
Each night to sleeping yards and happy wives and fear,
Without the blue chalk's fading bruise, the pint's dry foam
To mark our place, to call us back here, little waif
Who keeps the time, the time which cannot keep you safe.

A Message

Better, I guess, that you do not pick up
Tonight, since I have no real news, no hope
Of entertaining you. Everyone here's
Moved on by now, or grown old at the bars.
It used to be the two of us awake
At hours like this, the sidewalk wet and slack,
The traffic lights rehearsing absently.
Silly for me to wait on your reply.
Can you hear that—the siren whining past?
I wish just once the sound might be replaced
With music, something soft. Who wouldn't rather
Die to the blues? Chopin?
                                    One sound, another,
After a while I guess it doesn't matter . . .
Well, that was what I called for, to the letter,
Company for a couple blocks. I'm home.
The neighborhood's not bad. You ought to come.
Cafés, a park. It's prettiest in spring:
Trees blossom on the street and starlings throng
To every windowsill. Small children laugh . . .
Not really. I am drunk. I've said enough.
The empty sound of time recording time
Echoes across the phone line like a dream.
We'll have to talk more soon, or not at all.
We're getting late. It's old. I hope you call.

Prothalamium for My Father

I meant to write one for myself
Or maybe to compose a few
With irony for my regrets
Before devoting one to you,

But I've not met my better half,
And though you're not remarried yet,
Your fiancée puts up with you,
So take what comfort you can get.

You taught me what a promise means
When I was still in clip-on ties,
And once I'd learned to cinch the knot,
You promised every woman lies.

So maybe my astonishment
When you removed your wedding band
And let my mother find herself
Without your callused, helping hand

Was not mere filial surprise
At canceled vows and withered bliss
But shock at your acknowledgement
You'd been, in making do, remiss.

And whether your new courtship means
You've found a pleasant way to cope
With lifelong disbelief in love
Or something else, it gives me hope.

Heals-Gebedda

Make her a man's height   but mostly bone,
Naked, not half   the heft or shadow.
Grant her a mane   measured in armfuls,
The crown as dark   as the crook of her lap.
Bring to her neck   and nipples a flush
To slick her flanks   with salty tracks
Till her chin breaks   her cheek's promise
And her ring-hand takes   its rest in yours.
Think these parts   and her thought has come,
My way of life,   my wife, her sum.

Black Bile

for J.

If not for you, the day might have been lost,
So little of it mattered—just the play
Dawn cast across the blinds at no small cost
For morning, that had squandered last night's pay
On midday's glistening luck, though every ray,
Once you came home, broke off, as from a dream,
And like most easy fortunes passed away,
The motes unfastened from each wasted beam.
Probably to charge the world with any theme
Is vanity, or sentimental error.
Probably a life's less than it's made to seem,
A pricey suit mistaken for its wearer.
How happy, still, at dusk to talk about
The day with you I spent the day without.

The Open House

The smell of rain that night on old cement
Comes back to me, unlike the night, which can't,
We raced downtown past colds we should have caught
To see some place our friend had bragged about:

With marble steps ascending from the park,
And shelves in wood antique as it was dark,
An antebellum chandelier and view,
At bedside, of the monument. All true,

And all so nearly what we could afford,
Though we'd have liked a guest room. You demurred,
Descending to the street, and voiced some doubt
The sink or stove had roused, which you forgot

Among the ghosts of neighbors we would host,
Decades of coffee stains and burning toast,
The lullabies and tales we'd not yet penned,
And those blank years, without me, at the end.

Before a Wedding

Soon now the priest will call him in
And his happiness begin,

So, to make long seconds pass,
He surveys the colored glass

Picturing fond saints at rest
In their flames and cauldrons dressed,

Till the shade of one he knew
Wavers past his idle view,

One who married young and turned
Widow when the spring returned.

Come to wisdom thus, she taught
Boys like him who dimly sought

Wisdom at her ringless hand,
Someday soon to understand

Life and love for some have been
Lost and can't be tried again,

While impatient others fill
Empty seconds, happy still.

III.

Natural History

Complaint and treachery and disavowal
All find their places in the peerless files
Our microbes keep. No sigh or stifled howl
Goes missing from the list their staff compiles.
Emblazoned on the retina of the sun,
Each glancing infidelity endures.
The ocean's glare forgives not even one
Of our reflections, vain as fishing lures.
Footprints remarking every drunken step
Outlast the rain cloud's rant, the flaccid wind,
Stamped into storied dust as on a map
That leaves each atom, once uncertain, twinned.
And olden days, all long since cast aside—
Though we no more shall meet, yet they abide.

For the College Football Mascots

Here on the balding, bannered earth, your will is done.
Our lightfoot boys have armed themselves with your good name
Against this public moment. For your sake they pin
Fast by his wheeling arms helmeted time.
Beaten, he crawls, he falters, he pretends defeat—
For us, not you. You watch it all, huge, incomplete.

Half-animal, half-man, you thrive, kith of no kin,
Your body half-alive until the season's end,
The half-death of each pampered beast you've lived within.
Nothing of you is whole, no victory can mend
The undefeated fact, *mascotto*, meaning witch,
Our superstitions formed you, stitch by cunning stitch,

Though now you wait beyond our ken, beyond our forms,
To cheer and to be cheered in turn, gesticulating
Bravely, a king who guides his kingdom to the worms.
Coarse as the Cretan bull, the Hebrew calf, awaiting
Pitiless judgment, snorting blank October air,
You lurch past painted, quaking girls, their soft legs bare.

They understand the freight of you, the impotence
You suffer, staring out through great, cartoonish teeth.
They leave the stadium at night in sweats and glance
Back only briefly, if at all. The dark beneath
The rows of seats and empty beer cups thrums with you,
The dark one of these girls will send her son into.

Anvil Way

Here in the suburbs, twilight
Settles like a spell
Casting itself on winter.
For a moment, all is well,

As from the chalky steps
Climbing to the door
Of an idle student's home
I watch a labrador

Lope across the field
By the Presbyterian church
Until a boy's thin cry
Recalls it from its search.

Soon, when someone answers
The doorbell, I'll go in.
The children will leave off playing,
The crickets will begin.

When It Happens

When it happens, nobody seems to notice.
Someone coughs and hammers a nail through drywall.
Boys fling sticks at birds while the church bells tattle.
   Nightfall approaches.

When it happens, dog walkers trail their shadows,
Swing their sacks of waste through the tattered sunset.
Whitened breaths come loose into burnt October,
   Heady as incense.

Someone falters, pushing a drowsy infant
Up the sidewalk, touched by a breeze from childhood
Warm against the cheek as a shower in springtime,
   Full of misgiving...

Just perfumed exhaust from a neighbor's laundry,
Nothing special, nothing to tell the other
Babysitters after the playground's stumbled
   Into the darkness.

When it happens, all of the words are taken.
Those you might have called on, that could have helped you,
Rattle in the gutter on flyers and leaflets
   Selling you something.

Lamps supply each row house's upper windows
Heat enough and light to pretend it's morning.
Night's a looking glass in the fragile instant
   No one is looking.

Middle Age Toasts the End of Youth

Wait, put your hand down. Listen at least until
The struck match stutters. Everything after that—
    The smoke, the black street, all the strangers
  Lifting a bottle to greet you—will wait.

Alone it finds you. Pain you forgave yourself
Flares out of absence, singeing the naked dark
    Where only you can give it body.
  Safe as you felt in your clothes, it's found you.

Things that you've chosen, unfiltered cigarettes,
Dayshifts hungover, drives home between your thumbs,
    Sunglasses, years of fucking, friendships,
  All of them seemed to be chosen for you.

Look where the blown clouds shimmer like stolen dew.
No less than they have, you've been selected for.
    Soon now you'll have to give your answer,
  Soon as the flame of the match goes silent.

Letter in a Bad Time

for R.

The light has all but disappeared
Behind the bramble autumn's bared
    Across the roadside wood.
As I drive past at seventy
The dry scrub gives no thought to me
    But knits its own small good.

You sent a letter months ago
That silhouetted every woe
    And petty joy you tally
There on your abacus of ice
And bourbon, conjuring advice
    Upon each drink's finale.

Here, all the aimless, wheeling shapes
Of shadow-vines and shadow-grapes
    Shake out of sleep the past,
As distant images and names
Muddy the miles each county claims
    And each sign blurs the last.

Brother, I'm always leaving home,
And you are always finding some
    Reason to stay, to bear it
A little longer, something worth
Lashing that heart of yours to earth,
    That earth we won't inherit.

Late Aubade

i.m. Jane Pepperdene

When buried spring, in morning, wakes again
All winter's dreamless night has let remain,

Songbirds, returning north, will chart in song
A heaven crows have haunted all year long,

The rabbits' young will graze along a fence
Where honeysuckle slows the owl's advance,

Those buds curled damp against the dawn will glimpse
The automated snuffing of the lamps,

New-risen, naked day will spill its dew
While night grows parched and shadowy as you,

And on the hour the sundry church bells hallow
I will be pacing still this furrowed hallway,

At home where, though I speak, I can't but hold
My tongue, where you now never will be called

Back from choked roads, back from rivers sealed
With searing ice, back from the ashen field,

Back from the ceaseless season of the dead,
Where shadows till the dust their lovers shed.

Inaudible Elegy

Dumbstruck the afternoon I heard Mark Linkous
Had scissored through his life's indifferent knot,
I fell back, hard of hearing, on the hours
You and I listened, both awake and not,
To his soft music, taking it for ours.
Young still, those lisping songs are all that link us,

We who ruined sheets to "It's a Wonderful Life,"
The song, then the whole record, which we knew
Better than one another's mislaid clothes,
Who sprawled in loveless postures we thought new,
Talking of shades not lightly drawn to a close,
Like good George Bailey's in *It's a Wonderful Life*.

Such whispers through the past's thin walls I hear
Rarely now, though the skylit rooms we leased
Back then felt paid for, whitewashed, stationary
Shelters the brisk earth owed us. Not the least
Detail remains, not even the stationery,
On which I now write nothing. Take it, here.

The Homemaker's Song

Household things will hide themselves
In a task, like shade at noon—
Thimble, dust pan, tablespoon—
Less at home on idle shelves
Than in need, which comes too soon.

Widows

Though love prefers, unfailingly,
    Some rain-checked night less soon,
The wheezing heart's calliope
    To the pin-struck balloon,

It counts for little on the day
    The careering teacups halt,
When every height is turned away,
    Each looker-back to salt.

Along that disassembled earth
    Tossed memories skid along,
A beggar, tapping, weighs the worth
    Of the love in the song.

For the Highway Medians

I've known you only on the way to somewhere else.
Town of a girlfriend's parents. Airport. Mountain lake.
Often I picture my arrival, pleasing, false
As any plan, while I am driving on, and look
Briefly across your scrub and scattered, threadbare trees,
Deserted island in a narrow, man-made breeze.

Nobody's destination, you're inhabited
From time to time as something other than yourself:
A blind for idling state police, a watershed
For those who've turned back after getting only half-
Way home, the windy promise of an hourly wage
Someday for orange-suited cons, a softer cage.

Human, these passing needs are never truly you,
You whom we cannot help but pass eventually
And in our passing make you what you are—a few
Moments of peace, the brush, the field, the bright debris
Of wildflowers hurled by wind and honeybee from aisle
To grassy aisle. You are the spell, the little while.

Pretty and plain, you litter all my memories
Of family trips in childhood. Droning hours went by
No sooner if I marked each tree than otherwise.
Still, I'd number the trunks against the dimming sky,
The window's slicing edge. Although it raced to sever
Each one in turn, the farthest did not pass, not ever.

Nowhere

i.m. Steve Sigur

The sprinkler system wakes up on the hour,
Casting its vacant arcs across the lawn.
All night its clockwork tends to every flower
Bedded down here to bury roots and spawn,
While nowhere in particular my friend,
Who just last week lay mumbling on a cot,
Is dead, is nothing time or work can mend,
Though his machinery remains to rot
As I walk late at night across a campus
Hundreds of miles away, which is to say
As near to him as anywhere, and *tempus
Fugit* no less *irreparabile*
From me than from the blossoms here and there
Who do not know their lot, and do not care.

Miss Americus

City of Americus, Georgia

I should have visited by now
The town your mother said she knew
You'd never end up calling home,
Although it fit, from neck to hem,

Much like the dress she handed down
That made a show of what she'd done
Before your time, back in the place
That lent her flowers, a sash, and peace.

You wore her gown for Halloween
The year we very nearly won
Some contest, though I'd no disguise
Except your arm and smiling gaze.

I held them both, until in bed
You, talking of the future, bared
Your body's lavish wants, its plans
For faster friends, untaken pains.

A daughter of your own was not
Among your hopes, at least that night.
At least with me, and though we laughed
Together for a while, you left.

I miss that laughter now, the way I love
A life I write about but do not live.

First Love's Divorce

The day a student turned up late
With taut, red cheeks and truant eyes
And sat in studied calm until
The black-haired boy, a reprobate,
Took note and went to sit alone,
Well clear of where the girls would fill
Their desks with libel on his name,
I spotted in his face my own
Wish for the kid you should despise
To meet the teacher he became.

Your wedding news arrived not long
Before your rumored choice to part,
Or lack of choice. I heard both ways,
And neither seemed exactly wrong,
But when I caught a student sending
Across the room the same lost gaze
You once sent me, when I had done
Enough to spoil our hoped-for ending,
I saw there'd be no second start
And gave the lesson I'd begun.

Priam's Dream

Strange to wake, cheeks wet with someone else's tears,
Sleep leaving the room to morning's gold body
As my youth's old, dreamed-of ambergris goes sour
And I know my age before I know the day.
Not Sunday, but that other one, the last one...
It doesn't matter. I'll lie here either way
Till the glow under the bathroom door's winked out
And her shadow's worried over my eyelids
And she's passed into the kitchen's dull future.
Alone then, free of her looking, I will stretch
My silk-draped, ruinous legs to the cool floor.

Even an old man can still piss for himself,
Can still heft his organ, thick in a veined hand
And pass his own strong water unassisted.
Some days, at least, he ought to be able to.
Today he's not. I wash my hands anyway,
Lined hands in the ageless water, the same hands,
The same drawn, grizzled loins, the same blue-streaked calves,
The same wreck, now, as that smiling hag, my wife.
When was it we bargained to be left with this?
This nothing? We fed and coupled and wanted
For nothing until we woke, our cheeks wet, old.

And only, it seems, three thousand years ago
I was shielding my sun-glazed, kingly features
With a stranger's cowl and leaving home's high walls
For wet sand where my son's corpse lay, a trophy.
It fell to me, alone—a king, but alone—
To cross the blood-streaked seagrass with all the gold
Two strong mules could pull, against the night's quick hours,
Against the wishes of my wife—fragile still,
But firm-jawed and clear when she shows men her eyes.
And so I go, an old man grown old nobly,
Past hefting the sword but not being put to it,

And I keep my feet when a boy's figure glides
From the earth-drawn clouds into the wagon's path.
Watching his spear-head, I clutch my stick and smile,
Gentle as a host, and talk about my son,
About the long injuries and the ransom
And my good boy's altars, prayers mingled with blood
Under the gashed bull, foam-white limbs shuddering,
And as I name these to the golden stranger,
This soldier not yet grazed by a shaving knife,
It heals, that terrible, bronze-cut myth, my life,
And I feel myself, irreparably, made whole.

At the Spring Ballet Exams

Kirov Academy of Ballet, Washington, D.C.

It's here they've come, the graces and the gods,
Unwinged, to flutter through the mortal room,
Not with the girls who'll leap above the odds
Their classmates slipped beneath while in the womb,
Nor shadowing the pink-faced amateurs
Still swaying when the others stop or go
And sick with love no life of teaching cures,
A love now come to rest in the back row,
But here, where haloes flicker through the host
Whose form is clean and strong and nothing more,
Whose eyes have seldom risen to a boast,
Whose fates, like ours, lie mainly in the *corps*.
Among these pale, imperfect nine or ten
Retires the dream that heaven's always been.

Matthew Buckley Smith was born in Atlanta, Georgia. He earned his MFA in poetry at the Johns Hopkins University. His poems have appeared, or will soon appear, in various magazines, including *Beloit Poetry Journal, Commonweal, Iron Horse Literary Review, Measure, The Alabama Literary Review, Think Journal,* and *Best American Poetry 2011*. His poetry has been nominated for a Pushcart Prize. He lives in Baltimore with his wife, Joanna.

photo by Sarah Whitmeyer

www.ingramcontent.com/pod-product-compliance
Lightning Source LLC
Chambersburg PA
CBHW022149090426
42742CB00010B/1437